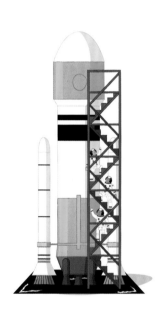

Note to parents, carers and teachers

Read it yourself is a series of modern stories, favourite characters, traditional tales and first reference books written in a simple way for children who are learning to read. The books can be read independently or as part of a guided reading session.

Each book is carefully structured to include many high-frequency words vital for first reading. The sentences on each page are supported closely by pictures to help with understanding, and to offer lively details to talk about.

The books are graded into four levels that progressively introduce wider vocabulary and longer text as a reader's ability and confidence grows.

Ideas for use

- Begin by looking through the book and talking about the pictures. Has your child heard this story or looked at this subject before?

- Help your child with any words he does not know, either by helping him to sound them out or supplying them yourself.

- Developing readers can be concentrating so hard on the words that they sometimes don't fully grasp the meaning of what they're reading. Answering the quiz questions at the end of the book will help with understanding.

For more information and advice on Read it yourself and book banding, visit **www.ladybird.com/readityourself**

Book
Band
5

Level 1 is ideal for children who have received some initial reading instruction. Stories are told, or subjects are presented very simply, using a small number of frequently repeated words.

Special features:

Opening pages introduce key subject words

Space words

space

rocket

International Space Station

spacesuit

astronaut

8

9

Large, clear labels and captions

Careful match between text and pictures

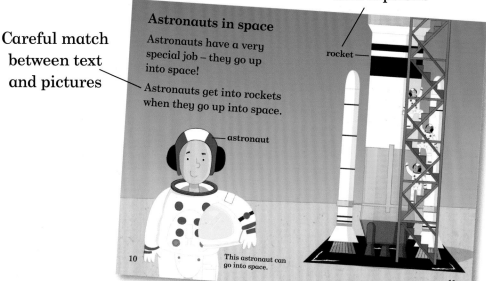

Astronauts in space

Astronauts have a very special job – they go up into space!

Astronauts get into rockets when they go up into space.

rocket

astronaut

10

This astronaut can go into space.

11

Educational Consultant: Geraldine Taylor
Book Banding Consultant: Kate Ruttle
Subject Consultant: Colin Stuart

LADYBIRD BOOKS

UK | USA | Canada | Ireland | Australia
India | New Zealand | South Africa

Ladybird Books is part of the Penguin Random House group of companies
whose addresses can be found at global.penguinrandomhouse.com.

ladybird.com

Penguin
Random House
UK

First published 2015
003

Copyright © Ladybird Books Ltd, 2015

Ladybird, Read it yourself and the Ladybird logo are registered or
unregistered trademarks owned by Ladybird Books Ltd

The moral right of the author and illustrator has been asserted

Printed in China

A CIP catalogue record for this book is available from the British Library

ISBN: 978-0-723-29504-4

Astronauts

Written by Catherine Baker
Illustrated by Max Powell

Contents

Space words

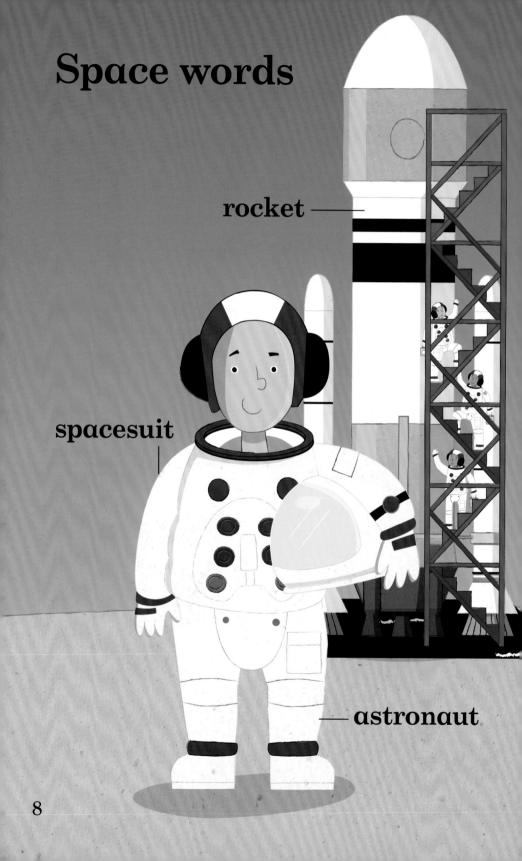

rocket

spacesuit

astronaut

space

International Space Station

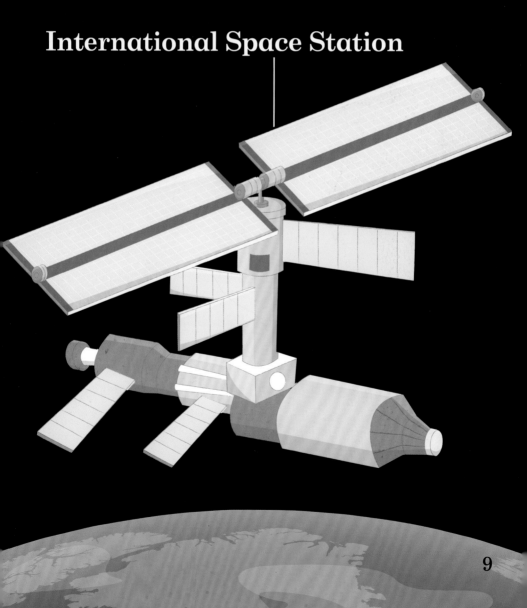

Astronauts in space

Astronauts have a very special job – they go up into space!

Astronauts get into rockets when they go up into space.

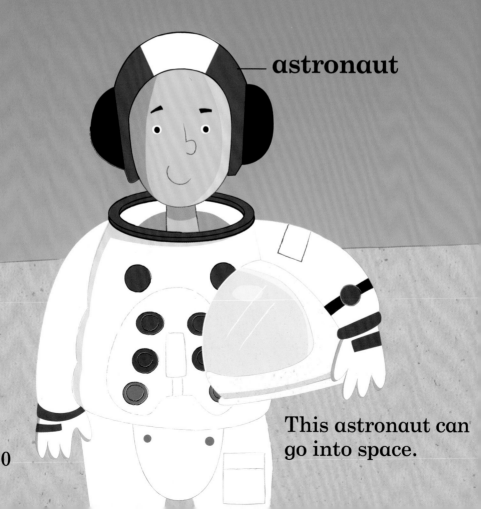

— astronaut

This astronaut can go into space.

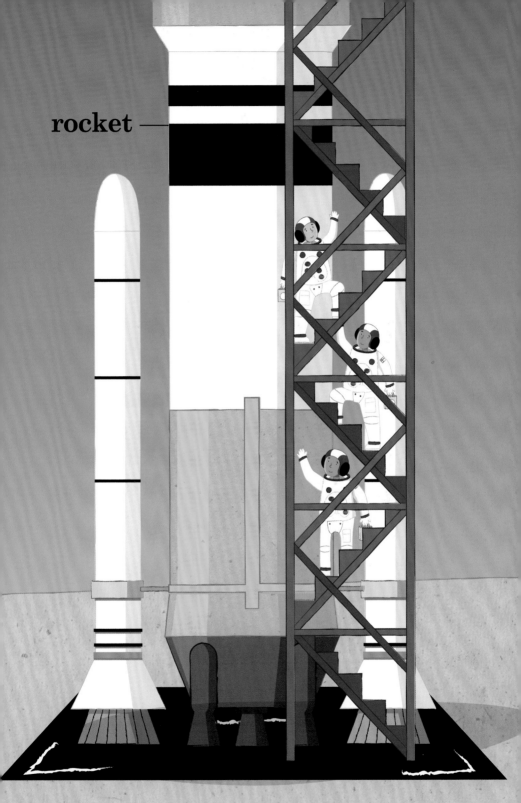

rocket

In a rocket

Rockets go up into space like this!

This rocket can go up into space.

These astronauts go up
into space in this rocket.

space

The International Space Station

Astronauts go up into space in a rocket to the International Space Station.

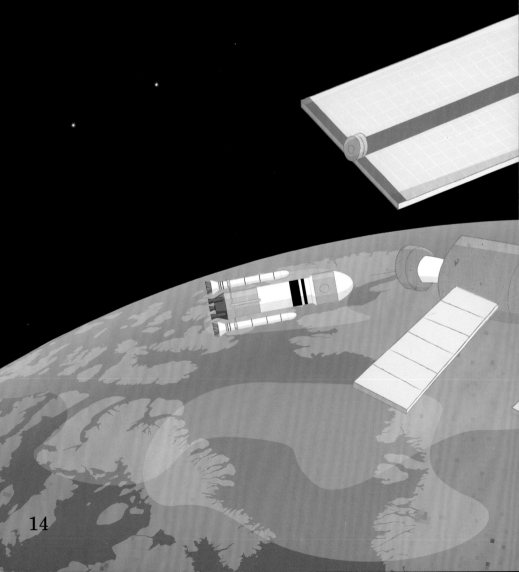

International Space Station

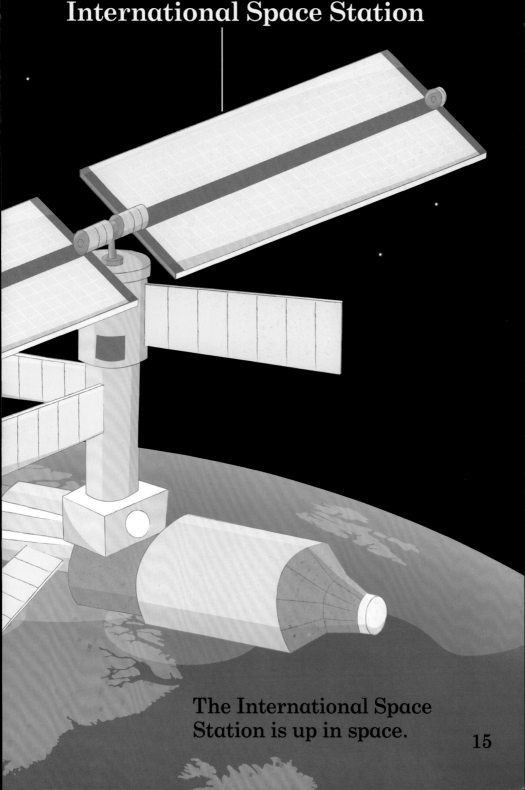

The International Space
Station is up in space.

Jobs in space

Astronauts do special
jobs in the International
Space Station.

Astronauts do not have spacesuits on in the International Space Station.

Astronauts in the International Space Station.

Spacesuits

Astronauts get
spacesuits like this.

This astronaut has
a spacesuit on.

spacesuit

Astronauts have spacesuits on when they do special jobs out in space.

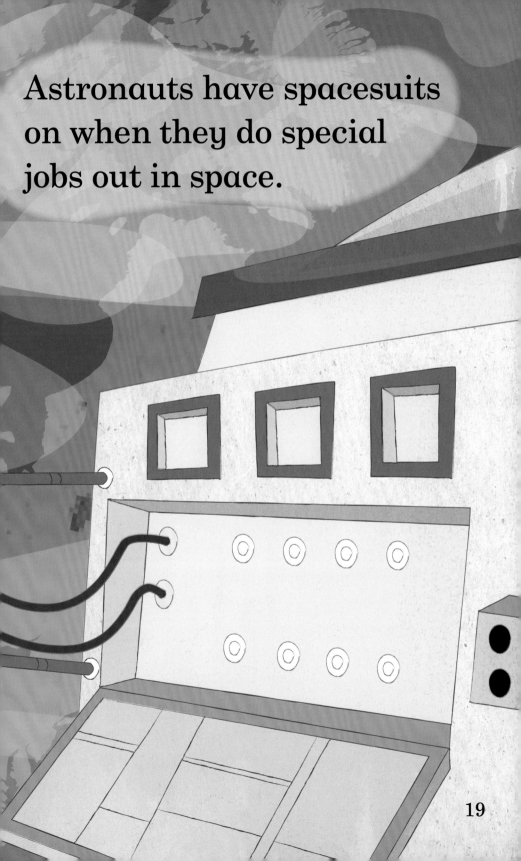

Astronauts float

Astronauts float out
in space.

This astronaut can float.

Astronauts float in the International Space Station.

Space food

Astronauts have very special food.

Astronauts get special food like this.

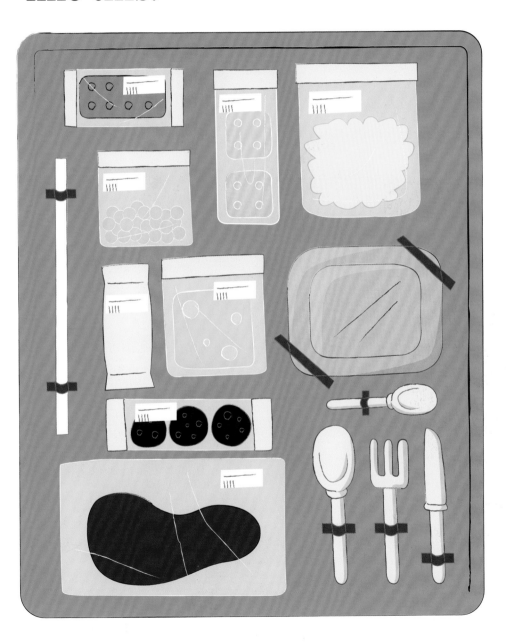

Astronauts exercise

Astronauts have to exercise in space.

These astronauts exercise in the International Space Station.

Astronauts shower and sleep

Astronauts have to shower and sleep in space.

— shower

This astronaut has a shower in the International Space Station.

Astronauts go to sleep like this!

Picture glossary

 astronaut

 exercise

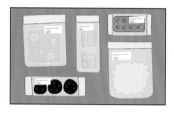 food

 International Space Station

 job

 rocket

 shower

 sleep

 space

 spacesuit

Index

Astronauts quiz

What have you learnt about astronauts? Answer these questions and find out!

- How do astronauts get into space?

- What do astronauts put on in space?

- Can astronauts float in space?

Tick the books you've read!

Level 1

Level 2

The Read it yourself with Ladybird app is now available